The elephant is the largest land animal. The largest ones weigh about 12,000 pounds.

Elephants weigh more than 200 pounds
when they are born. They are about
3-1/2 feet tall.

Elephants are smart animals. They have very good memories.

An elephant can use its trunk like a
very strong arm.

An elephant can also use its trunk to pick up small, delicate objects.

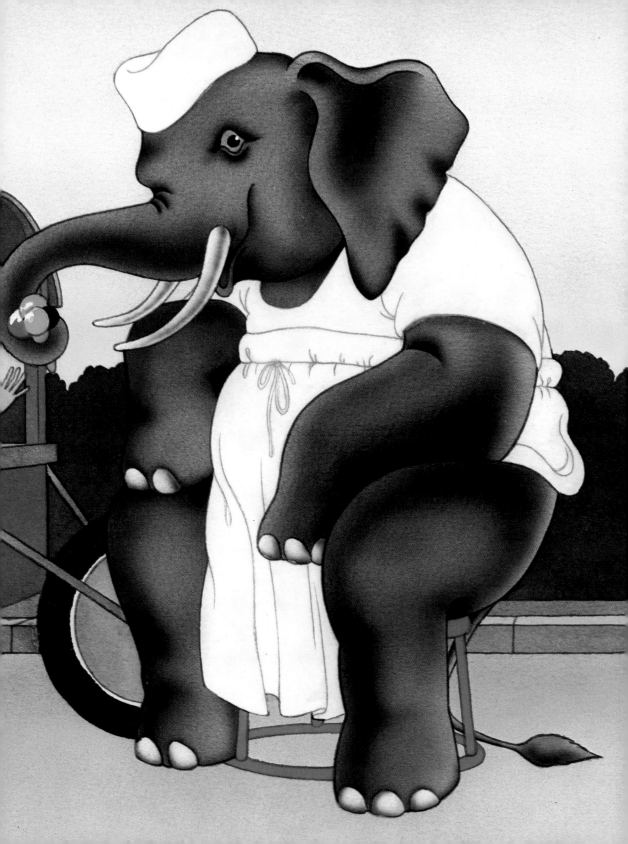

Elephants live in large herds.
Sometimes old male elephants
go away to live alone.

An elephant needs to eat about 600 pounds of vegetables and drink about 40 gallons of water every day.

Elephants love to swim and take baths. They will travel far to find enough water.

After bathing, elephants throw
sand or dirt on themselves to
protect their skin from insects.

Elephants were important
animals in wars long, long ago.

Asian elephants are smaller than African elephants and can be easily tamed.